GW00481796

And When You Pray...

ELISABETH ELLIOT

GATEWAY
TO JOY

BOX 82500
LINCOLN, NE 68501

And When You Pray

Bible verses are quoted from *The New Testament in Modern English* (J. B. Phillips)

The Good News Broadcasting Association, Inc.
3000 printed to date—1992
(5-8457—3M—22)
ISBN 0-8474-1194-X

Cover photo: Four by Five

Printed in the United States of America

I grew up not in that great company of Christians who traditionally used written prayers, but among those who believed that prayer was not real, that it was not sincere unless it was impromptu. One's own words, and only one's own, would reach heaven. There was a single exception to this rule: what is commonly called the Our Father or the Lord's Prayer. This one we memorized at home long before we could read, and repeated daily in family prayers following the extemporaneous prayer our father offered.

Once when I was a little girl I was shocked to see a minister praying in the pulpit with his eyes open. I of course was caught with mine open—I who had been taught always to pray with bowed head and closed eyes. But here was a man of God, not staring at his congregation, which would have been bad enough during a prayer, but actually reading from a piece of paper. It seemed he had prepared his congregational prayer, just as he had prepared his sermon.

It took me years to overcome my suspicions and to understand not only the necessity of a prayer book to guide people in their worship together, but the legitimacy of a preacher's reading a prayer, possibly even one written by somebody else.

It did not take me quite so long to

realize that in my private devotional life I needed help in knowing what and how to pray. If I knew of specific needs of others I mentioned them, for we are plainly told to make our requests known to God. That God knows what they are before we have spoken or even thought of them is obvious, but God wants to be asked. Prayer brings us to the Father.

A father knows much better than the children what they really need. Many of our requests to our heavenly Father, like those of any child to his earthly father, are silly. We don't see them as silly or we would be ashamed to ask. We see them as good, right, necessary, desirable. But as we grow in grace we learn to pray (almost honestly), "Thy will be done in earth, as it is in heaven." That means, "Answer only those prayers, Lord, which will accomplish *your* loving and eternal purposes, not my selfish and temporal ones." Think what a mess things would be, not only in our own lives but in the world, if every prayer sent up to God were answered. Thank God, He often says no—because He is sovereign, which means He is Lord of all; because He orders the universe according to an everlasting covenant; and because He loves us.

Let us never forget, when we pray, that things which are impossible with men are possible with God. This is because He is all-powerful. But let us remember, too, that some things that are possible with men are impossible with God. This is because He is all-loving. What men call love is often nothing more than a feeble and indulgent sentiment. Human love excuses where it ought to forgive, gives way where it ought to hold like steel, soothes where it ought to pierce. The love of God is a white heat, pure, fierce, and strong enough to save the world. Therefore, to answer the desperate cry of the Son of Man, "If it be possible, let this cup pass," was not possible. It was a prayer that could not be answered, for it was impossible for the Father to save the world and save the Son at the same time. The world's life depended on the Son's death. The Father gave His Son. The Son gave Himself to death. That is love.

We do not see very far when we pray. We are thinking, feeling, acting, dreaming, imagining, desiring, scheming creatures. We come to God with all our thoughts, feelings, actions, dreams, imaginings, desires and schemes. They limit and color and shape (and certainly often corrupt) our prayers. It is immeasurable comfort, then, to know that "the Spirit also helps us in our present limitations. For example, we do not know how to pray worthily, but his Spirit within us is actually praying for us in those agonizing longings which cannot find words. He who knows the heart's secrets understands the Spirit's intention as he prays according to God's will for those who love him" (Romans 8:26, 27).

Is it possible at all to "pray worthily"? I think there are some prayers in the Bible which can guide us to the sort of thing God wants us to ask. They may at first seem too exalted. We may feel that it would be hypocrisy to pray such prayers. As we pray them, however, setting our sights always higher and higher for those we love, we can rest assured that the Spirit of God is helping us in our present limitations. We pray "in Jesus' name"; so we want what we ask to be in line with what He would want.

Years ago it happened that I had a long list of names to pray for, but I hardly knew what to ask. They were the names of Indians who had lately become Christians. I was perhaps the only person praying for some of them, and I knew little of their real needs. I began to use the prayers I found in J. B. Phillips's *Letters to Young Churches*, copying them into the little notebook where I kept my lists. I asked for them just what Paul had asked for the new believers of Corinth, Colosse, Thessalonica and such places. The words, written so long ago by the inspiration of the Holy Spirit, seemed to encompass all the truly important things I wanted to ask for the people of Shandia and Arajuno and Puyupungu. There was a clarity, a power, an immediacy which surprised me.

It is my earnest hope that many who are not accustomed to the use of a prayer book will find help in taking these words of Scripture, praying them first for themselves, and then inserting into them the names of people they want to lift up to God. It may be useful to compare your own petitions with the petitions of these written prayers. Note how often such things as love, knowledge, fruit, strength, joy and thanksgiving are mentioned. May it be that the things on your list are the "raw material" out of which God will produce the things on Paul's list? There is unquestionably a correlation between the ordinary events of our lives and the fruits of holiness which God wants to give us— we need to work, and God wants to give us strength; we find ourselves in trouble, and God wants us to learn patience; life brings sorrow, but the joy of the Lord comes as a gift of grace; we enjoy all kinds of pleasures, and our hearts swell with thanksgiving. Let your prayers take into account both aspects: the human situation that you would naturally pray about, and the divine gift that will sanctify it.

"If they are our own words they will soon, by unavoidable repetition, harden into a formula. If they are someone else's, we shall continually pour into them our own meaning" (C. S. Lewis, *Letters to Malcolm,* New York: Harcourt, Brace & World, 1964, p. 11).

Prayers

Romans 15:5, 6, 13

May the God who inspires men to endure, and gives them constant encouragement, give you a mind united with one another in your common loyalty to Christ Jesus. And then, as one man, you will sing from the heart the praises of God the Father of our Lord Jesus Christ. . . . May the God of hope fill you with all joy and peace in your faith, that by the power of the Holy Spirit, your whole life and outlook may be radiant with hope.

Ephesians 1:16-19

I thank God continually for you and I never give up praying for you; and this is my prayer. That the God of our Lord Jesus Christ, the all-glorious Father, will give you spiritual wisdom and the insight to know more of him: that you may receive that inner illumination of the spirit which will make you realise how great is the hope to which he is calling you—the magnificence and splendour of the inheritance promised to Christians—and how tremendous is the power available to us who believe in God.

Ephesians 3:14-21

I fall on my knees before the Father (from whom all fatherhood, earthly or heavenly, derives its name), and I pray that out of the glorious richness of his resources he will enable you to know the strength of the Spirit's inner re-inforcement—that Christ may actually live in your hearts by your faith. And I pray that you, rooted and founded in love yourselves, may be able to grasp (with all Christians) how wide and long and deep and high is the love of Christ—and to know for yourselves that love so far above our understanding. So will you be filled through all your being with God himself! Now to him who by his power within us is able to do infinitely more than we ever dare to ask or imagine— to him be glory in the Church and in Christ Jesus for ever and ever, amen!

Philippians 1:9-11

My prayer for you is that you may have still more love—a love that is full of knowledge and wise insight. I want you to be able always to recognise the highest and the best, and to live sincere and blameless lives until the day of Christ. I want to see your lives full of true goodness, produced by the power that Jesus Christ gives you to the glory and praise of God.

Colossians 1:9-12

We are asking God that you may be filled with such wisdom and that you may understand his purpose. We also pray that your outward lives, which men see, may bring credit to your master's name, and that you may bring joy to his heart by bearing genuine Christian fruit in all that you do, and that your knowledge of God may grow yet deeper.

And When You Pray . . .

Colossians 4:12

Epaphras, another member of your Church . . . prays constantly and earnestly for you, that you may become mature Christians, and may fulfil God's will for you.

1 Thessalonians 3:9-13

How can we thank our God enough for you, and for all the joy you have brought in the presence of our God, as we pray earnestly day and night to see you face to face again, and to complete whatever is imperfect in your faith? So may God our Father himself and our Lord Jesus guide our steps to you. May the Lord give you the same increasing and overflowing love for each other and towards all men as we have towards you. May he establish you, holy and blameless in heart and soul, before God, the Father of us all, when our Lord Jesus comes with all who belong to him.

1 Thessalonians 5:23, 24

May the God of peace make you holy through and through. May you be kept sound in spirit, mind and body, blameless until the coming of our Lord Jesus Christ. He who calls you is utterly faithful and he will finish what he has set out to do.

2 Thessalonians 1:11, 12

We pray for you constantly, that God will think you worthy of his calling, and by his power may fulfil all your good intentions and every effort of faith. We pray that the name of our Lord Jesus may become more glorious through you, and that you may share something of his glory—all through the grace of our God and the Lord Jesus Christ.

2 Thessalonians 2:16, 17

*May our Lord Jesus Christ and God
our Father (who has loved us and
given us unending encouragement
and unfailing hope by his grace) in-
spire you with courage and confi-
dence in every good thing you say or
do.*

2 Thessalonians 3:5, 16

May the Lord guide your hearts into ever deeper understanding of God's love and of the patient suffering of Christ. . . . Now may the Lord of peace personally give you peace at all times and in all ways. The Lord be with you all.

1 Timothy 2:1-3

Supplications, prayers, intercessions, and thanksgivings should be made on behalf of all men: for kings and rulers in positions of responsibility, so that our common life may be lived in peace and quiet, with a proper sense of God and of our responsibility to him for what we do with our lives. In the sight of God our saviour this is undoubtedly the right way to pray; for his purpose is that all men should be saved and come to know the truth.

Philemon 6

I pray that those who share your faith may be led into the knowledge of all the good things that believing in Christ Jesus means to us.

Hebrews 13:20, 21

Now the God of peace, who brought back from the dead that great shepherd of the sheep, our Lord Jesus, by the blood of the everlasting agreement, equip you thoroughly for the doing of his will! May he effect in us everything that pleases him through Jesus Christ, to whom be glory for ever and ever. Amen.

2 Peter 1:2

May you know more and more of grace and peace as your knowledge of God and Jesus our Lord grows deeper.